wireless WISE KIDS

Safer ways to use mobile and wireless technology

By Lyn McLean, BA Dip Ed, B Ed
Illustrated by Janet Selby, B (Art) Ed

First published 2012
Reprinted 2015

Published by Envirobook on behalf of
EMR Australia Pty Ltd.

PO Box 347, Sylvania Southgate NSW 2224
Phone: 02 9576 1772
emraustralia.com.au

Copyright © 2015 Lyn McLean and Janet Selby

All rights reserved.

ISBN-13: 978-1479215843

Edited by Sarah Evans

Typesetting by Bungoona Technologies

To Jacqueline and Alexandra,
Lily and Blacky the cat

What do mobile phones, cordless phones, laptops and tablets have in common?

They send information through the air without using any wires.

This information travels through the air in tiny packets of energy carried by microwave radiation.

Even though you can't see, hear or smell this microwave radiation, it's always present when wireless devices are sending or receiving information.

You might hear this information as a voice or see it as pictures, but it reaches you in just the same way.

Here's how it works.

When Sam calls Kate, Sam's mobile phone adds the information from his message to a signal of microwave information.

His phone's aerial sends this radiation into the air.

The microwave radiation reaches a mobile phone base station which might be on top of a building or on a tall metal tower.

The base station sends the message on until it reaches a base station near Kate and this base station sends it to Kate's phone.

Kate's phone changes the information carried by the microwave radiation into the sound of Sam's voice.

Cordless phones, tablets and computers also use microwave information.

Microwave radiation travels back and forth between the

cordless phone and its base

 wireless computer and its modem

tablet and a base station.

Microwave radiation travels through solid objects such as walls. This is why you can use a cordless phone in a different room to the base or you can use a laptop in a different room to the modem.

goes through walls

This means that microwave radiation can travel into a person's body.

The amount of microwave radiation from a mobile phone that is absorbed by a person's brain is called the Specific Absorption Rate (or SAR) of the phone.

Phones with higher SARs can have more effects on a person's body.

Many people think it's a good idea to keep the amount of microwave radiation entering a person's body as low as possible.

Here are some ways you can do it.

If you're buying a new mobile phone, buy one with a low SAR rating.

You can find this out from the user manual or by contacting the manufacturer.

Don't spend longer than you need to on your mobile phone. Just use it for important messages and don't use the internet with it.

Keep your phone turned off as much as possible.

If you use your phone for games, turn your phone to airplane mode while you play.

Don't hold your mobile phone right against your head. Instead, here are some things you can do.

Text rather than call.

Use speaker phone.

Use a headset.

It's especially important to keep your phone away from your head when you're dialing a number because the phone puts out more microwave radiation then than when you're talking.

Don't keep your mobile phone next to your body, like in your pocket, when it's turned on.

Instead you can:

Turn your phone off when you're not using it.

Put it in a bag.

Don't use your phone in a low reception area

like a car

or a lift.

In a low reception area, the phone has to work harder and it sends out more microwave radiation.

better reception

You can tell when you're in a low reception area from the bars on your phone. The more bars, the better reception it has.

Keep your mobile phone away from your bed.

Don't sleep with it under your pillow.

Don't use it as an alarm clock.

Don't charge it next to your bed because the charger may also be harmful.

Cordless phones are just like mobile phones because they send and receive information using microwave radiation.

In a cordless phone, microwave radiation comes from

the handset

and the base.

Some cordless phones give out microwave radiation all the time, even when no one is making a call!

Don't spend too long talking on a cordless phone.

Less time

Make sure the base of a cordless phone is not near your bed or desk.

too close

Phones with wired connections don't give out microwave radiation, so they are much safer.

no waves

Wireless computers connect to the internet with microwave radiation. This radiation travels back and forth between the computer and the modem.

Don't forget, it can pass through walls and even a person's body.

Don't spend too long using a wireless computer.

Make sure the modem isn't near your bed or desk.

too close

Turn off the modem when no one's using the internet.

Don't work with your laptop on your lap.

Wired internet connections don't use microwave radiation.

If you use wired connections, don't forget to turn off the wireless connection!

Tablets connect to the internet with microwave radiation.

Don't spend longer on the internet than necessary.

Make sure your tablet is on airplane mode when you play games.

Don't rest your tablet on your body when you're using the internet.

Using wireless devices safely is a smart thing to do!

LYN MCLEAN

Lyn McLean has been investigating and writing about electromagnetic radiation (EMR) since 1996. She is author of 'The Force – living safely in a world of electromagnetic pollution', published by Scribe (2011). She is publisher of the quarterly report 'EMR and Health' and has written many published articles on EMR.

Lyn was Deputy Chair of two committees that developed and updated the Australian telecommunications code on mobile phone base stations and was a long-term member of the Australian Government's EME Reference Group. She ran the EMR Association of Australia for nine years and is currently Director of EMR Australia PL.

She is a former teacher with extensive experience working with children of all ages.

Lyn can be contacted at www.emraustralia.com.au.

JANET SELBY

Janet Selby is an artist of diverse talents. She is an illustrator, sculptor and ceramic artist, who has exhibited her work in a wide range of locations.

Janet is illustrator of the popular Australian children's book 'Bindi-eye Bop' whose unique and colourful bush characters delight children as they sing along to the tunes in the accompanying CD.

Janet trained as a high school art teacher and now holds regular workshops for people of all ages.

She can be contacted at www.janetselby.com.au

Made in the USA
Monee, IL
17 July 2021

73785060R00024